All to Your Glory

Poetry for God Lovers

All poems written in this book have been inspired by God's Word (the Bible); Creation in all its wonders, and perhaps what I call 'heavenly nudges'.

I give all the glory to God and ask Him to Bless those who read these verses.

Sandra Catherine Stanton

All photographs presented in this book were taken by the author

Printed in Victoria, BC, Canada

Note for Librarians: a cataloguing record for this book that includes Dewey Decimal Classification and US Library of Congress numbers is available from the Library and Archives of Canada. The complete cataloguing record can be obtained from their online database at: www.collectionscanada.ca/amicus/index-e.html
ISBN 1-4120-4496-0

TRAFFORD

This book was published *on-demand* in cooperation with Trafford Publishing. On-demand publishing is a unique process and service of making a book available for retail sale to the public taking advantage of on-demand manufacturing and Internet marketing. On-demand publishing includes promotions, retail sales, manufacturing, order fulfilment, accounting and collecting royalties on behalf of the author.

Offices in Canada, USA, UK, Ireland, and Spain
book sales for North America and international:
Trafford Publishing, 6E–2333 Government St.
Victoria, BC V8T 4P4 CANADA
phone 250 383 6864   toll-free 1 888 232 4444
fax 250 383 6804   email to orders@trafford.com
book sales in Europe:
Trafford Publishing (UK) Ltd., Enterprise House, Wistaston Road Business Centre
Crewe, Cheshire CW2 7RP UNITED KINGDOM
phone 01270 251 396   local rate 0845 230 9601
facsimile 01270 254 983   orders.uk@trafford.com
order online at:
www.trafford.com/robots/04-2304.html

10   9   8   7   6   5   4   3   2

This book is dedicated to my family who I love so much, for their help in making a dream become a reality. First thanks go to my son Andrew for all his hard work in preparing the artwork and for his belief in this project. To Jennifer, my sister-in-law who had the original vision for the book and it's layout.

Special thanks go to my husband Philip who supports me in all I do, for his patience and commitment.

Thanks of a unique kind go to my daughter Linzi, son-in-law Shaun and my beautiful grandchildren, Maya, Esme and Kester. They touch my heart to write in ways they are totally unaware of.

My brothers, Pat and Kevin, have helped to move me forward in my writing life by their kind and loving appreciation of my work.

I am so grateful to Sarah who has been supportive and spiritually' in tune' with all I do. Thanks for your inspiration for the poem 'Walking', it blesses my heart.

Finally thanks to so many special friends who have encouraged me along the way, I name but a few... Ken and Amanda, David and Helen, Audrey, Maria, Olwen, Mila, Nettie, Carol, Bex and dear Maggie Mou my unofficial poetry manager!

In all your ways know, recognize,
and acknowledge Him, and He will
direct and make straight and plain
your path.

(Amplified Bible) Proverbs 3 v 6

ALONE WITH GOD

CONSUME ME LORD

AWAKE O SLEEPER

I COME RUNNING

MY HEART IS AWAKE

SACRED STILLNESS

BEYOND MY REASON

SHADES OF SERENITY

MAKE MY HEART A GARDEN

WALKING

ETERNAL PARACLETE

WATER JARS OF HEAVEN

THE HAND OF ALL SOLACE

PENITENT DREAMER

PRECIOUS

But we have the mind
of Christ (the Messiah)
and do hold the thoughts
(feelings and purposes)
of His Heart.
(Amplified Bible) 1 Cors. 2 v 16b

Alone With God

Alone with God, what a precious delight
A conscious discovery of His Holy Light
It bathes me gently, yet with piercing dart
Captivating, enveloping, my openness of heart

A hand covers mine, we walk, we stand
Beside the Red River that cuts through this land
I'm taken, broken, blessed and forgiven
Divinely filled and Spirit driven

With the ear of faith I hear His voice
Resounding, echoing, a singular choice
Always to listen, always to see
With the Mind of Christ given to me

This heavenly realm is always in sight
When longing pulsates to reach Shekinah height
Here fig tree bears fruit alongside blossoming vine
For I am my beloved's and He is mine

He will fulfil the desires of
those who reverently and
worshipfully fear Him; He
also will hear their cry
and save them.

(Amplified Bible) Psalm 145 v 19

Consume Me Lord

Bright lights before me are slowly appearing
An inhale of holiness is in my breathing
The Glory of God is entering my being
Responding to cries of desperate pleading

I feel, I touch, I know you're here
Abba, Jesus, Holy Spirit, you're near
You fill my heart, my mind, my hand
All broken open, as before you I stand

I see your face looking down from the tree
Your eyes crying joy, in pain for me
Consume me Lord, come take control
Let every part now just gently unroll

I see my Shepherd's delight, as I become unwound
I'm laid out before Him, my face to the ground
Then in tender embrace I am lifted up high
Where I see my Saviour, now eye to eye

A tear falls between us, is it His or is it mine?
The aura is dazzling and from His face I shine!
It's the King of Kings, yet I'm in His arms
In His touch is healing, as He soothes and calms

I'm rendered speechless, I'm in total awe
I'm like a little child just wanting more
He tells me my desire is His greatest pleasure
And the Kiss of the Son is my own heart's treasure.

And be constantly renewed in the spirit
of your mind (having a fresh mental and
spiritual attitude) And put on the new nature
(the regenerate self) created in God's image,
(Godlike) in true righteousness and holiness.

(Amplified Bible) Ephesians 4 v 23-24

Awake O Sleeper!

Sweet dew of the night, God's holiness mist
Permeates my dreams, so I can not resist
The call of the morning, Christ's opening words'
Awake, O sleeper! Surely you've heard
How you shall arise, to where none can destroy
The sparkling light of heaven, my deep song of joy?'

Yes! Lord Come! Renew the spirit of my mind
Until Jesus within me is all that you find
Enable me to press in and outwardly progress
Your love and compassion, be all I express
Let mercy flow through me, so that all I'll convey
Is your fragrant perfume, throughout this new day

Root out from me Lord, sin's every dark trace
Covering all, with your cleansing pure grace
Cause me to grow like the beautiful Palm
Upright and steadfast, blessed by spiritual calm
Then even in a desert, a wilderness bare
I'll bring forth good fruit and be blossoming there

Mountains make a way and highways rise up
As I hunger and thirst for your sacred full cup
When this flower is fading, by your glory I'll be drawn
Knowing at each sunrise, fresh mercies are born
To rain down on me, like jewels from your crown
Giving peace to my heart, right through to sundown.

If I (can) speak in the tongues of men and
(even) of angels, but have not love, I am
only a noisy gong or a clanging cymbal.

(Amplified Bible) 1 Cors. 13 v 1

I Come Running

Here I am Lord, before your throne
Here I kneel Lord, all alone
If I'm a clanging bell, then bring to harmony
And write my prayer into sweetest symphony

Father you're Faithful, Righteous and True
And your burden is light, so I come to you
Sovereign Lord, we are bonded in love
And purest Spirit, you make everything good

I've come from a place that's dry and thirsty
To rest awhile at your seat of mercy
And between touching wings, I now behold
Holiness held open, by those angels of gold

You are The Way, the Everlasting Door
And I come running, to worship and adore
I hear the echoed cries of Jesus, upon Spirit breath
As I'm encompassed in freedom, brought by His death

Overwhelmed in gratitude my tears are falling
And all within me is thankfulness calling
Love, Light and Life, come fill my days
As you're with me always - to the end of the age.

Bless (affectionately, gratefully praise)
the Lord, O my soul! O Lord my God,
You are very great! You are clothed with
honour and majesty - Who makes the
clouds His chariot, Who walks on the
wings of the wind.
(Amplified Bible) Psalm 104 v 1, 3

My Heart is Awake

Come draw me, call me, away this day
Upon my lips whispering kisses lay
Ointment of Jesus come pouring forth
To issue a fragrance of endless worth

O divine perfume now hedge me in
To boundaries that allow only purity within
Even when asleep, my heart is awake
To this banquet of love of which I partake

If hardship mountains be ahead of me
Or sorrowing valleys down below I see
We'll walk on the wings of the wind together
And ride those chariot clouds forever

I'll know when the time for singing is here
When your voice is calling "Beloved come near"
All shadows will flee from among the flock
Whilst others will have lost their door to knock

The scent of my Saviour is deep inside
And from His gaze, I never shall hide
"You've ravished my heart," He says to me
So, to all that I am, He holds the key.

May my meditation be sweet to
Him; as for me, I will rejoice in the Lord.
(Amplified Bible) Psalm 104 v 34

Sacred Stillness

Beside still waters I sit in quiet contemplation
Waiting and watching in silent meditation
Through windows of my mind I begin to see
How precious, Lord, are your thoughts towards me

In sacred stillness I wait upon Him
All around becoming misty and dim
Making me aware of a nourishing stream
That fills my thoughts like a waking dream

You have searched me and know all there is to tell
So my deepest needs are dropped into your well
My soul is thirsting and my flesh now yearns
For your living water upon a heart that burns

Keep me always in this peaceful calmness
To see, then taste, your delectable goodness
Holy Spirit walk me through God's beauty arrayed
And upon this scene let my mind be stayed

O, let me linger in this place divine
Losing myself and all sense of time
Surrendered and drenched in such love sublime
Knowing the sweet hope of glory, Christ Jesus, is mine!

But God shows and clearly proves
His (own) love for us by the fact
that while we were still sinners,
Christ (the Messiah, the Anointed One)
died for us.

(Amplified Bible) Romans 5 v 8

Beyond My Reason

Jesus, lover of my soul and essential part
Of who I am and what fills my heart
Transport this child to some celestial height
Where the dance of angels will fill my sight

I hear your voice O Judah's Lion
Telling of the great golden City of Zion
Where sun nor moon will be shining bright
But the glory of God its brilliant light

I can see the One Upon the Throne
He holds my heart that once was stone
And tears fall down His lovely face
To mingle with mine like heavenly lace

Between His hands is a jar, exquisite and rare
My pain and sorrow contained in there
He holds the vessel with delicate care
Whilst His eyes melt all, in one compassionate stare

Lord, you love me far beyond my reason
With an intensity of feeling that has no season
But blows eternally through clouds of divinity
To surround and carry me into infinity.

As the heart pants and longs for the water brooks, so I pant and long for You, O God. My inner self thirsts for God, for the living God. When shall I come and behold the face of God?

(Amplified Bible) Psalm 42 v 1-2

Shades of Serenity

Down the narrow path through the coolness of evening
Walks an eternal child, of God's own gleaning
Longing to disrobe from the day's worldly dross
Here hang angel's baskets of heavenly moss

And the grass along this way does not wither
Where trusting the Lord, He calls us hither
Come dwell in my safe land, the choicest part
And I will give you my desires, for your own heart

He who makes your righteousness shine like the dawn
Will call you to be still on His chosen lawn
To feel the lush pastures enfold your feet
And in shades of serenity His Spirit you'll meet

Yearnings will break open before the Lord
Heart-felt pounding under Spirit's sword
But softly it falls upon shoulders bent
Submitted to the justice and tender mercy sent

Taken out from 'Egypt', carried upon eagles wings
This surrendered child, the Lord Himself now brings
Before the Father, beneath His gaze
To stand with Cherubim in this holy place

Falling at His feet, more dead than alive
A voice of rushing waters causes life to revive
The dew of heaven drops, from the Living One
Melting a heart… merging two into one.

(You have called me a garden, she said) Oh, I pray that the (cold) north wind and the (soft) south wind may blow upon my garden, that its spices may flow out

(Amplified Bible) Song of Solomon 4 v 16

Make my Heart a Garden

Make my heart a garden, where you can walk
In the cool of the day, together we'll talk
Tell me Father, how I used to live
In a land of shadows, where I couldn't forgive

How you broke each branch and lifeless they fell
The sickness, the sin, the darkness of hell
Like enemies scattered, like foes that fled
Past the foot of the cross, as my Jesus bled

Breathe through my garden on the wings of the breeze
Perfume my life as each leaf on the trees
Let all that has life feel the touch of the Son
And the moon for all seasons mark that day is done

Abba, Father, now speak of your peace
Pass all understanding, let joy increase
Leave a rainbow cover forever to glow
Consuming each flower of thought that I know

Christ is in me, what mystery divine
Praise to His glory, can all this be mine?
Oh! Living Hope – come Spirit like a dove
Rest in my garden, my God of all love.

Create in me a clean heart, O God, and
renew a right, persevering, and steadfast
spirit within me.
(Amplified Bible) Psalm 51 v 10

Walking

Beaten down by tempests of cold and heat
Exposed to the trampling of many feet
This path I walk is smoothed and worn
History's secrets trodden, from earliest dawn

As I tred this way, I begin to hear
The sounds of heaven coming near
God speaks to me, as I ask of Him
'Why is the light within me dim?'

Create in me an upright spirit
One that knows no earthly limit
Shape my soul to some fresh start
That brings new life into my heart

Branches each with blotchy stain
Are overhanging this narrow lane
Rough, then smooth, stripped of bark
Seasons of life that leave their mark

God shows me that He knows all
And once again, I can walk tall
I'm told to be, 'as gentle as a dove'
Asking for wisdom from above.

O magnify the Lord with me, and
let us exalt His name together.
(Amplified Bible) Psalm 34 v 3

The Eternal Paraclete

Come let us magnify the Lord, what a precious treasure
To worship and adore, within the stream of His pleasure
Pouring out our hearts before God the King
Glory and Majesty, is what we lovers sing

O God You are Our God, reigning on high
Earnestly we seek You, in awe we sigh
In the beauty of Your holiness we shall enter now
As Your rolling waves cover us, we willingly bow

From submissive wonder, bursts forth our praise
The total of our being, before You now lays
Here in Your sanctuary, this sacred holy place
The light of Your radiance is upon each eager face

The fool says in his heart that there is no God
Others who know Him are given the wings of a dove
To fly away, and rest, where the Lord is close
Led by the Helper, the blessed Holy Ghost

Star of Jacob, what is it that You give?
Everything to make these dead bones live!
Dwelling within, making us totally complete
Revelation truth declared, by the eternal Paraclete.

...I saw the Lord sitting upon a throne, high and lifted up, and the skirts of His train filled the (most holy part of the) temple. Above Him stood the seraphim; each had six wings: ...And one cried to the other and said Holy, holy, holy is the Lord of hosts; the whole earth is full of His glory!

(Amplified Bible) Isaiah 6 v 1, 2 and 3

Water Jars of Heaven

Fountain of light spring from inside
It's time, it's calling for me to decide
To create a sanctuary where God can dwell
Where secret wonders to me he'll tell

Open my heart, let bright stars fall
Awaken my soul to a devotional call
Into your temple, aware of your glory
Where six-winged angels cry out your story

Wrapped in your robe of unfailing love
Water jars of heaven are tipped from above
Quenching my thirst for all your delights
I taste, I drink, on wings take flight

Sailing the skies, just holding your hand
Gliding, soaring what creation you planned!
Almighty God is with me on high
Taking me deeper, my fulfillment is nigh

My heart steps out, it's the pathway of peace
My soul so serene in thankful release
My mind now set on those heavenly places
Never to hinder God's current of graces

My eyes will see, revelations my goal
Lips now cleansed with forgiveness coal
Always I'll look with expectant eyes
Knowing my Lord, all flesh now dies

I push open the gates, pass the mercy seat
I see the Lamb, I hear His bleat
"Surrender, surrender, come fall at my feet
I'm you're all in all, your vision complete."

When I view and consider Your heavens, the work of
Your fingers, the moon and the stars, which You have
ordained and established, What is man that You are
mindful of him, and the son of (earthborn) man that
You care for him?

(Amplified Bible) Psalm 8 v 3-4

The Hand of all Solace

Slowly I stroll under wavering trees
Through dappled lighting from moving leaves
These lights dance around like stars at my feet
Enticing my steps, to my place of retreat

Here the sun is drying the glistening pool
Left by a shower, that came to cool
Where honeycomb rings, small bubbles of froth
Are like an embroidered pattern, upon a delicate cloth

Across the fields are rippling earth waves
Mounds of lush grass that beautifully behaves
Like a waltzing breeze, so gently blown
A soft velvet carpet of every green tone

Above the meadow, on pitted rocks I stand
Knowing all was formed at His great command
Around me, flower filled moss spreads far and wide
Like a spectacular seaweed, across a hilltop tide

The azure blue ocean encircles my view
In awesome wonder.... Oh! what can I do?
But release my praise, cry out in adoration
Give all that I am, to the One of perfection

Here, as I look to God and seek His face
Come within His presence, in this secret place
I see Him beckoning, 'Come near and see'
As the hand of all solace is offered to me.

(Roaring) deep calls to (roaring) deep at the thunder of Your waterspouts; all Your breakers and Your rolling waves have gone over me. Yet the Lord will command His loving-kindness in the daytime, and in the night His song shall be with me, a prayer to the God of my life.

(Amplified Bible) Psalm 42 v 7- 8

Penitent Dreamer

Angel whispers brush the furrows of my mind
Ministering to the aches that are hiding behind
Those smiles, the calm, the positive words
That I have spoken from all that I've heard
Promises that assure all will be fine
As I look to Jesus and know that He's mine

When I ponder on thoughts that bring a frown
I'll seek His face, watch His love come down
Falling from heaven in words pure and true
To keep and guard me, tasting mercies anew
And my heart awakens to sweet communion with Him
Where eyes of faith widen, knowing He's forgiven all sin

God, come touch, make whole, this penitent dreamer
I will meditate on You, My Rock and My Redeemer
And my feet will become sure, able to stand
Like a deer on the heights of some wilderness land
Establish my steps Lord, as I heed Your right way
Open up my understanding to all that you'd say

By streams of water I will prosper and learn
Being like a tree, now planted so firm
And in peace, I'll both lie down and sleep
Knowing your saftey through deep calling deep
Sometimes stilled and by the small voice led
Down the roads of my life in the years ahead.

O Lord, you have searched me (thoroughly) and have known me. You know my downsitting and my uprising; You understand my thought afar off. You sift and search out my path and my lying down, and You are acquainted with all my ways. For there is not a word in my tongue (still unuttered), but, behold, O Lord, You know it altogether. (Amplified Bible) Psalm 139 v 1-4

Precious

Lord you have healed me through and through
So here I am to give honour to you
I stand, I turn, to look into your face
Knowing you have left not even a trace
Of unfinished work within my soul
You've supplied every need that can make me whole

The battle is won, I'm crucified with Christ
There's no turning back and no time to waste
Forward is the way, so onward I should go
His redeeming blood, through my veins can flow
Giving strength to my mind and depth to my spirit
I can soar with the eagles and know no limit

Now I know, what I did not see
Those pierced hands that cradled me
The veil has gone, now I'm so deeply conscious
Of how the Lord My God has named me 'Precious'
He covered me, even within my mother's womb
Then walked beside me under sun and moon

His perfect knowledge of me is immeasurably great
The number of His thoughts to me, I'm unable to state
And I know my 'Preciousness' in Him will not fade
Because He says, that I am so wonderfully made
Created in His image...His divine workmanship
So I surrender all, to His Sovereign Lordship

Before me now I see a most fertile plain
Where I can grow and blossom under my given name
'Precious!' O 'Precious!' God has called unto me
Giving reason to my birth and who I'm meant to be
My way has been paved with all riches in glory
In Jesus it was finished, yet not the end of my story

For my eyes need to see and my ears need to hear
The fullness of my salvation, through my God given years
I remember how He chose the foolish, to confound the wise
And lifted those who are weak, giving strength as their prize
So now I can do all things, in Christ it is done!
Always and forever, led by the Light of God's Son.

Sandra Catherine Stanton was born in Derby, England. She left school at 15 years old with no particular qualifications but a love of English language. As a mature student at Southampton University, England, she gained an honours degree in Psychology.

Currently living on the Island of Cyprus in the Mediterranean with husband Philip, they have a son Andrew and a daughter Linzi,
two young granddaughters,
Maya and Esme, and a small grandson, Kester. Sandra Catherine feels that her writing is a very precious time with God and prays that all who read these verses will be blessed.

**All proceeds of this book will be used to
help street children across the world.**

www.inspirationalverses.com